5 STEPS ENGLISH

The Happy Prince

낮은 단계부터 원문까지 한 권에 담은

단계 영어 행복한 왕자

초   판| 1쇄 발행 2022년 10월 24일
개 정 판| 1쇄 발행 2024년 01월 17일

원 작 자| 오스카 와일드
영어번역| 스티브 오, 주디 고
그   림| 김연희
정보맵핑| 이야기 연구소
디 자 인| 아름다운디자인
감   수| HannahAllyse Kim / Jinny Lee
제 작 처| 다온피앤피
특허출원| 10-2020-0012558
국제출원| PCT/KE202/002551

펴 낸 곳| ㈜도서출판동행
출판등록| 2020년 3월 20일 제2020-000005호
주   소| 부산광역시 부산진구 동천로 109, 9층
이 메 일| withyou@withyoubooks.com
홈페이지| withyoubooks.com
카카오톡| @동행출판사

단계별 요약정보 기술은 국내특허출원 및 PCT 국제출원을 받았습니다.

ISBN 979-11-91648-13-3
ISBN 979-11-91648-11-9 (세트)

낮은 단계부터 원문까지 한 권에 담은

단계 영어

(행복한 왕자)

동행
WITHYouBooks

영어 실력이 자랄수록
영어책도 진화해야 합니다.

자녀 신발이나 옷 사주실 때 한 치수 큰 거 사주시죠? 금방 자라니까요. 아이의 머릿속 사고도 금방 자랍니다. 사고가 자랄수록 영어책도 자라야 합니다.

어린 나뭇가지를 방치하면 제멋대로 구부러지고 휘어 자랍니다. 반대로 어릴 때 누워있는 가지를 세워서 곧은 부목을 대고 실을 감아 놓으면 그대로 반듯하게 자랍니다. 아이도 똑같죠. 매번 나무를 뽑아 버리고 더 큰 나무를 새로 심지 마세요. 하나의 나무를 키워나가게 가르치세요. 이 책은 하나의 스토리를 수준에 맞게 5단계로 발전시켜 나가는 신개념 영어 도서입니다!

한 번 아이들이 말을 배우는 과정을 생각해 보세요. '엄마', '아빠'와 같이 몇 안 되는 단어만 말하던 아이가 시간이 지나면 말이 길어지고 내용이 깊어집니다. 그러니까 처음엔 "엄마 밥 줘" 였는데, 시간이 지나면 "엄마 내가 좋아하는 김밥 먹고 싶어요" 처럼 표현에 깊이가 생긴다는 것입니다. 하지만 여기서 중요한 사실은, 표현은 달라졌지만 말하고자 하는 핵심 내용은 같다는 것입니다. 둘 다 "음식을 먹고 싶다 (또는 배고프다)"는 게 핵심입니다.

단계 영어 구성은 마치 아이들이 3~4년에 걸쳐서 언어가 성장하는 과정을 레벨 1~5에 넣은 것과 같습니다. 레벨1이 4살 아이의 표현이라면, 레벨2는 5살 아이의 표현이라 볼 수 있습니다. 전달하고자 하는 핵심 내용은 원문과 같지만, 그것을 표현하는 방식이 레벨에 따라 달라집니다.

계단을 오르듯이 레벨별로 한 번 읽어보시기를 바랍니다.

Steve Oh

As your English skills grow, English books should evolve accordingly.

When you buy shoes or clothes for your child, you probably buy them one size larger? Because they are growing up. Thought in the mind of a child grows quickly, too. As the thought grows, English books should grow together.

If young twigs are left unattended, they will grow bent and crooked. On the other hand, if you support a branch which lies on the earth by putting a straight splint on it, and winding a thread, it will grow straight as it is. The child is the same. Do not pluck a tree every time and plant a new tree, which is larger. Teach them to grow a tree. This book is a new concept English book that develops a story in 5 stages according to the level of the reader!

Think of the process of children learning to speak. A child who used to say only a few words such as 'mom' and 'dad' can utter longer words and their speech comes to have deeper meaning as time passes. So, at first they say "Give me food, Mom", but as time goes on, the expression becomes more complicated, like "Mom, I want to eat my favorite food Gimbap". But the important point here is that the intention of the speech is the same, although the words are different. The fact is "I want to eat (or I'm hungry)".

The composition of I Can Read English is as if we put the course of language development of children over 3 to 4 years into the level of 1 to 5. If Level 1 is the expression of a 4-year-old child, Level 2 is the expression of a 5-year-old child. The core content they want to convey is the same, but the way they express differs depending on the level.

I hope you read it once for each level as if you were climbing the stairs.

Steve Oh

독자후기

"
출발이 쉬워 좋습니다. 레벨이 오를 때마다 "같은 내용을 이렇게 다르게 표현하네."라고 말하게 됩니다. 살짝 게임을 하는 느낌도 나네요.

— 천호동 JOY

"
단계 영어책은 신세계입니다. 특히 영어에 자신 없으신 분들께, 영어 포기했다고 생각하시는 분들께 강력히 추천하고 싶어요. 한 단계씩 읽어나가다 보면 어느새 마지막 단계에서 자연스럽게 책을 읽고 있는 자신을 발견하실 수 있으실 거예요. 제가 그랬거든요. 아이에게 동화책 읽어주듯이 소리 내 읽으면 그 효과가 배가 되는 것 같아요. 레벨1, 2는 쉽지만, 너무 중요한 단계더라고요. 내용을 연상하며 다른 사람에게 이야기할 수 있을 정도 꼼꼼히 읽고 나면 레벨 3도 어렵지 않게 되고요. 이렇게 레벨3까지 성공하면 레벨4, 5에서 사전 없이도 자연스럽게 책이 읽혀요.

— 천안시 엠제이

"
쉬운 내용으로 반복해서 읽을 수 있다는 게 가장 좋은 부분이고 그걸 반복하니까 다음 단계로 넘어가기도 수월한 것 같아요.

— 등촌동에서 호균

"
영어 실력이 유아보다 못해서 1단계 읽을 때 이해가 되어 좋았고 점점 단계가 높아지니 어려워진다는 걸 느끼지만 아~ 이렇게 내용이 자세하게 변하는구나, 읽다 보니 이해가 되고 내용을 알 수 있게 되어서 정말 신기하고 좋았습니다. 꾸준히 해야겠다 느꼈고 사실 동화로 하니 신났습니다. 특히 1단계는 아이도 좋아해서 읽어주면 무척 잘 듣고 신나 하더라고요. 영어를 어렵다고 무조건 겁낼 게 아니라 도전해 보자 하는 마음이 들었고 주변에도 추천해주고 싶습니다. 계속 단계별 읽기를 해서 영어 읽기 실력을 높이고 싶어요. 단계별 영어 동화 계속 만들어 주세요~

— 기장군 윤우 엄마

"
읽기도 도움이 많이되었고, 특히 글의 확장을 단계별로 배울수 있는게 특히 더 도움이 많이 되었어요.따로 단락을 나눠서 글을 써봤는데, 한눈에 알아보고 공부하기도 더 좋았구요.

— 익명의 서포터

"

It's easy to get started. Every time your level goes up, you'll think, "Wow, we can describe the same thing in such a different way." I feel like I'm playing a game.

- JOY

"

An I Can Read English book is a new world. In particular, I would highly recommend it to those who are not confident in English, and to those who think they have given up English. If you read it step by step, you will find yourself reading the book naturally at the last step. It happened to me. If you read aloud just like reading a children's book for a child, I think the effect is doubled. Levels 1 and 2 are easy, but they are very important steps. After reading carefully enough to recall the content and talk to others, you will feel level 3 is difficult. If you succeed up to level 3 in this way, you can read books naturally at levels 4 and 5 without a dictionary.

- MJ

"

The best part is that it is easy to read and can be read over and over again. I think it's easier to move on to the next step because of this repetition.

- Hogyun

"

My English is really poor and probably not better than a toddler, so it was good to have an easy boo. I feel good because I could understand when I read the Level 1 book. I feel that it gets more difficult as the level goes up. But I could sort out how the expressions changed. As I read it, I was able to understand and comprehend the content, which was really interesting and good. I felt I had to keep doing, and I was really excited to do it as a fairy tale. Especially in the first stage, my children also like it. They listen to me and enjoy it. Instead of being afraid of speaking English because it is difficult, I decided to try it, and I would like to recommend it to those around me. I want to improve my English reading skills by continuing to read step by step. Please keep making "I Can Read English".

- Yunwoo's Mom

"

It helped me in reading and it was especially helpful in that I could learn step-by-step extension of the text. I wrote the article in separate paragraphs, and it was better to read and study at a glance.

- Anonymous supporter

독자후기
Reviews

"영어 공부를 해야 하는데... 라는 생각을 하던 중 대학생 때 교수님이 영어도 언어이기 때문에 초급부터 시작하는 게 좋다며 원서를 읽는다면 영어 동화책부터 시작해서 차근차근 공부해보라는 이야기가 떠올라서 알아보던 중 단계 영어를 알게 돼서 가벼운 마음으로 시작했어요. 우리나라에서도 번역으로 알려진 동화라 전체적인 줄거리는 알고 있는 상태에서 레벨1을 읽으니 옛 기억을 조금씩 떠올렸고, 가급적 쉬운 단어와 단순한 문장으로 조금 수월하게 읽었던 거 같아요. 레벨2부터는 대충 이런 내용이겠거니... 하며 추측하며 읽을 수 있었습니다. 원서에 대한 막연한 두려움이 있어서 쉽게 시작하지는 못하고 있었는데 단계별 영어 동화를 통해 한 걸음 내디뎠습니다. 앞으로 출간될 도서들로 공부해서 영어에 친숙해지도록 노력해보려고요. 좋은 책 출간해 주셔서 감사합니다. 앞으로도 잘 부탁드릴게요.

- 봉덕동 지연지현

"Level 1을 보면 이것쯤이야 하고 시작하게 됩니다. 쉬운 영어 읽기로 첫 level을 읽고 한 권의 내용을 이해하니 level 2에서 단어가 하나 늘어나도 쉽게 유추가 되고 책이 읽힙니다. 그렇게 단계를 업하다 보니 마지막 원서까지 다섯 권의 책을 보게 되었네요. 혼자서 한 권의 영어책을 처음 읽어봤어요. 매일 chapter 한 장씩을 읽다 보니 생활에 영어책 읽기가 습관화되고 한 권을 다 읽었다는 성취감이 다음에 어떤 영어책을 읽을 수 있을까 기대되고 새로운 책도 도전하고 싶습니다.

- 양평군 안윤경

"학창 시절부터 영어 공부를 어느 정도 해왔다고 생각하는데 말하기와 듣기는 상대적으로 실력이 잘 늘지 않았습니다. 단계별 영어 동화는 기존에 제가 가지고 있던 부담감을 조금 덜어 주어서 좀 더 편하게 공부할 수 있었던 거 같습니다. 쉬운 단계부터 시작해서 기초를 쌓고 어려운 단계로 넘어가서 연계해 나가는 배움이 즐거웠던 거 같습니다.

- 물금읍 소율 아빠

"
While I was thinking that I should study English... I remembered that my professor said that it is better to start at the beginner level because English is also a language, when I was a college student. The professor recommended to start from English fairy tales to read English books. While I was looking for easy books, I came to know this I Can Read English, and I started with a light heart. As it deals with well-known fairy tales through translated version in Korea, I could recall my old memory while reading Level 1. It consists of simple words and simple sentences as much as possible, so I could read it easily. From level 2 onwards, I read it by guessing what it would be like... It was not easy to start because I had uncertain fears about the reading an English book, but I took a step forward through an I Can Read English. I will try to become familiar with English by studying books that will be published in the future. Thanks for publishing a great book. I wish you all the best in the future.

– Jiyeong and Jihyeon

"
When you first encounter Level 1, you can start reading with light heart, thinking that it is easy. Even if number of words increase one by one in level 2, you can easily infer the content and read the book without much difficult, because you have already read the Level 1 books. As you progress like that, you will finish five books up to the last one. It was the first time I read an English book by myself. As I read chapter by chapter every day, reading English books has become a habit in my life, and I am looking forward to what kind of English book I can read next, and I want to challenge myself with a new book.

– Ahn Yungyeong

"
I thought that I have been studying English to some extent since I was a student, but my speaking and listening skills have not improved relatively well. I Can Read English relieved the burden I had in the past, so I was able to study more comfortably. I think it was fun learning to start with the easy level, build the basics, and move on to the difficult level.

– soyul's Dad

사용설명서
Manual

영어는 언어입니다. 언어는 암기보단, 실제 사용을 통해 익혀야 합니다. 즉, 의미가 있어야 하고 내가 사용해야 합니다. 이 책은 학습지가 아닌 책으로서 영어를 의미 있게 사용할 수 있게 제작했습니다.

간단 하지만 명확하게 도서 사용 방법을 말씀드리겠습니다.

① 영어 공부가 아닌 **책을 읽는다고 생각**하세요.

② **레벨 1부터 읽으세요.** 레벨 1이 무척 쉽게 보여도 일단 레벨 1부터 읽어야 다음 단계로 수월하게 올라갈 수 있습니다. 마치 계단을 오를 때, 첫 계단에 발을 내디디고 그다음 계단으로 오르는 것처럼 말입니다.

③ **모르는 단어가 보이면 사전[1]을 찾지 마세요.** 다시 한번 말씀드리지만, 이건 책입니다. 책은 읽어야 합니다. 우리가 보통 책을 읽을 때 국어사전을 찾으면서 읽지 않는 것처럼 말입니다.

④ **레벨 5까지 읽었다면 이제 레벨 4, 3 순으로 거꾸로 읽어 보세요.** 복잡한 문장들이 어떻게 간략하게 요약되는지를 배울 수 있게 됩니다.

사용법은 위 4가지면 충분합니다.
자, 그럼 이제 시작해 볼까요?

---

[1] 레벨5 에서는 사전을 찾으셔도 됩니다. 내용 이해를 위해서가 아닌 모르는 단어의 정확한 의미 파악을 위해 사전을 찾을 필요가 있습니다.

English is a language. Language should be learned through practical use rather than memorization. That means, it has to make sense and you have to use it. This book is not a study book, but a book designed to use English in a meaningful way.

I will tell you how to use the book in a simple but clear way.

1. Do not think that you study English. Instead, read the book.

2. Read the book from level 1. Even if level 1 looks very easy, you should read level 1 first to move up to the next level with ease. It's just like climbing the stairs. When you go upstairs, you place your foot on the first stair and then go up to the next one.

3. If you see a word you don't know, don't consult a Dictionary. Again, this is a book. The book must be read. It's just like we don't consult an English dictionary when we usually read an English book.

4. If you have read all the way to level 5, now read books backwards in order of level 4 and 3. You will learn how to concisely summarize complex sentences.

If you have learned above 4 methods, it is sufficient.
So, let's get started, shall we?

목 차
Contents

오디오북
채널

Happy Prince **LEVEL 3** 99

Happy Prince **LEVEL 4** 155

Happy Prince **LEVEL 5** 195

5 Steps English
The Happy Prince

LEVEL 1

1,105개
단어(Words)

186개
문장수(Sentences)

4분 25초
읽는 시간(Reading Time)

8분 30초
말하는 시간(Speaking TIme)

5.9
문장 길이(Sentence leangth)

LEVEL 1

행복한왕자 레벨1

Chapter 1

The Happy Prince is Loved

There was a Happy Prince.

The Happy Prince had a golden body.

14

The Happy Prince had blue eyes and a sword.

People loved the Happy Prince.

People always talked about the Happy Prince.

The Happy Prince looked happy.

Chapter 2

The Little Swallow and the Reed

One night, a Bird came to the city.

The Bird did not go to the warm place.

The Bird loved the beautiful Grass.

"I love you," the Bird said.

The Bird stayed with the

Grass.

"This is foolish," said the other birds.

In the fall, the other birds flew away.

The other birds left. The Bird was lonely.

"Will you come with me?" the Bird said to the Grass. But the Grass said, "No."

"Goodbye!" the Bird flew away.

Chapter 3

The Little Swallow and the Happy Prince

The Bird came to the city. The Bird saw the Happy Prince. The bird sat near the Happy Prince.

The Bird was sleeping. Rain fell on the Bird.

The rain fell on the bird again.

"I want a better place," said the Bird.

The rain came down again and again.

The Bird looked up. The Happy Prince was crying.

"Who are you?" the Bird said.

"I am the Happy Prince."

"Why are you crying?" the Bird asked.

"I was a prince. I was never sad. Now I am dead. I can see everything in the city. I can see sad things. I am sad," said the Happy Prince.

Chapter 4

The Ruby from the Sword

"There is a poor house. A woman is working there. Her son is sick. Bird, take the stone out of my sword. Give it to them," said the Happy Prince.

"My friends are waiting for me," said the Bird.

"My friends are in the warm place. They are playing by the river. They are talking to the flowers," said the Bird.

"Bird," said the Prince, "stay with me. They need help."

"I don't like boys. I met two boys before. They threw stones at me," said the Bird.

The Bird saw the Happy

Prince. The Happy Prince looked sad. The Bird was sad.

"I will stay here," said the Bird.

"Thank you," said the Prince.
The Bird took the stone. The Bird flew away. The Bird saw the church.

The bird saw the palace.

People danced in the palace.

The Bird saw a woman and
a man.

"I want to see my dress
soon," the woman said.

The Bird saw the ships.
The Bird saw the shops.
The Bird came to the house.

The Bird put the stone in the house.

The Bird went back to the Happy Prince.

"I feel warm," said the Bird.

"You are warm because you helped someone," said the Prince.

Then the Bird slept.

Chapter 5

The Sapphire from the Eye

In the morning, the Bird went to the river. A person saw the Bird. He was surprised.

"It is winter. But there is a bird!"

"Tonight, I will go to the warm place," said the Bird.

The Bird met other birds.
The Bird had a good time.

At night, the Bird went to
the Happy Prince.
"I am leaving," said the
Bird.

"Bird, stay with me," said
the Prince.

"My friends are waiting
for me," said the Bird.

"Bird, there is a young
man in the city. He is at

a desk. He is writing. But he is too cold. He is very hungry," said the Prince.

"I will stay with you. I will give him a red stone," said the Bird.

"I don't have a red stone. Take my eye stone," said the Prince.

"I can't do that," the Bird cried.

"Bird, please do it," said the Prince.

The Bird took the eye stone. The Bird went to the man.

The Bird gave the stone to him.

"Someone gave this stone to me," said the young man.

He looked happy.

In the morning, the Bird went to the sea.

"I'm going to the warm place!" said the Bird.

At night, the Bird went to see the Happy Prince.

"Goodbye," the Bird said.

"Bird, stay with me," said the Prince.

"It is winter here; I will come back in the spring," the Bird said.

"There is a girl in the city.

She sells matches. She is crying. Take my other eye stone. Give it to her," said the Happy Prince.

"I will stay with you again. But I can't take your eye," said the Bird.

"Bird, please do it,' said the Prince.

The Bird took out the eye stone. The Bird went to the girl. The Bird gave the stone to her. The girl was happy.

The Bird went to the Prince.

"You can't see; I will stay with you," said the Bird.

"No, Bird, you must go," said the Prince.

"I will stay with you forever," said the Bird.

Chapter 7

The Gift for the Poor People.

The next day, the Bird told stories to the Prince. The stories were about the warm place.

"Bird, go to the city. Tell me about the people," said the Prince.

The Bird went to the city.

The rich people were happy.
But the poor people were
hungry.

The poor people were sad.

Then the Bird came back.
The Bird told the Prince
about the city.

"I have a golden body.
Take the gold. Give the
gold to the people." said
the Prince.

The Bird took the gold.
The Bird gave it to the
people. The people were
happy.

Chapter 8

The Death of the Swallow

The snow came. The streets were white.

The Bird was cold.

But the Bird stayed with the Prince. The Bird loved the Prince.

"Goodbye, Prince! I will kiss your hand," said the Bird.

"Kiss me on the lips. I love you," said the Prince.

The Bird kissed the Happy Prince. The Bird died.

Then the Happy Prince

died too.

In the morning, people saw the statue.

"The Happy Prince looks bad," they said.

"The red stone on the sword is gone. His eye stones are gone. His gold is gone!" said the people.

So they took away the statue
of the Happy Prince.

People put the Happy
Prince in the fire.

The people made
another statue.

"This is strange; the heart is not melting," said the work-man.

So they threw away the heart.

"Give me the most beautiful things in the city," said God.

An Angel gave Him the dead heart and the dead bird.

"Yes. This bird and the Happy Prince will be happy. They will go to heaven," said God.

5 Steps English
The Happy Prince

LEVEL 2

1,813개

단어(Words)

296개

문장수(Sentences)

7분 15초

읽는 시간(Reading Time)

13분 56초

말하는 시간(Speaking TIme)

6.1

문장 길이(Sentence leangth)

LEVEL 2

Chapter 1

The Happy Prince is Loved

A Happy Prince was in a city.
He was a statue. The Happy
Prince had a golden body.

He had two blue stones for his eyes and a red stone on his sword.

People loved the Happy Prince.

"The Happy Prince is beautiful. But he cannot do anything," the Town Leader said.

"Be happy! Be like the Happy Prince," said a mother to her child.

"I am happy. The Happy Prince is happy," said a sad man.

"He is an angel," said the children.

"You did not see an angel," said the teacher.

"We saw an angel in our dreams," said the children.

Chapter 2

The Little Swallow and the Reed

One night, a little Bird came to the city.
The Bird did not go to the warm place.

He loved the beautiful River Grass. He met the River Grass when he went to the river.

"May I love you?" said the Bird.

The Bird flew around the Grass. The Bird stayed with the Grass all through the summer.

"This is foolish love," said the other birds. "She has no money. And her family is very big."

In the fall, the other birds flew away.

The other birds left. The Bird was lonely. The bird was tired of love.

"The Grass does not talk to me," the Bird said.

"The Grass is always at home. But I love traveling."

"Will you come with me?" the Bird asked the Grass.

But the Grass said, "No." She

loved her home.

"You do not love me," the Bird cried.

"I will go to the warm place. Goodbye!" and the Bird flew away.

Chapter 3

The Little Swallow and the Happy Prince

The Bird came to the city. The Bird saw a statue.

"I will stay here," he said. The Bird sat near the Happy Prince's feet.

"Look at this gold," the Bird said. He went to sleep.

The rain came down.

"This is strange!" he said. "There is no clouds in the sky. But it is raining."

The rain came down again.

"I am getting wet. I want a better place," the Bird said.

The rain came down again and again. The Bird looked up. The Bird saw the Happy Prince's eyes. The Happy Prince was crying.

"Who are you?" the Bird said.

"I am the Happy Prince."

"Why are you crying?" asked the Bird. "You made me wet."

"I was a prince. I was never sad because I lived in a palace. I played in the garden. I danced in the hall. I was beautiful. People called me the Happy Prince. I was so happy. Now I am dead. I can see everything in the city. I can see bad things. I can see sad things. That is why I am crying," said the statue.

Chapter 4

The Ruby from the Sword

"There is a poor house," said the statue.

"The window is open. I can see a woman. She is sewing. She has a sick son. He wants oranges.

But she has nothing. Bird, take the red stone

out of my sword. Bring it to them. I can't move."

"My friends are waiting for me in Egypt. They are flying near the river. They are talking to the flowers. They sleep on a large grave," said the Bird.

"Bird," said the Prince, "stay with me for one night. They need help."

"I don't like boys. I was near the river last summer. There

were two boys. The boys always threw stones at me. They were not kind to me," said the Bird.

The Bird saw the Happy Prince. He looked sad. The Bird was sad too.

"It is very cold here. But I will stay for one night," said the Bird.

"Thank you, Bird," said the Prince.
The Bird took the red stone

from the sword. The Bird flew away.

The Bird saw the church. The Bird saw angel statues.

The Bird went to the palace. People danced in the palace. The Bird saw a woman and a man.

The woman was beautiful.

"I want to see my dress soon. A woman is making my dress. But she is so slow," the woman said.

The Bird saw the lamps on the ships. The Bird saw the people at the shops. The Bird came to the house. The boy was in bed.

The mother was so tired. The Bird put the red stone on the table.

The Bird went back to the Happy Prince.

"It is cold, but I feel warm now," said the Bird.

"You are warm because you did something good. You helped someone," said the Prince.

Then the Bird went to sleep.

Chapter 5

The Sapphire from the Eye

In the morning, the Bird went to the river. A Science Teacher saw the Bird. He was surprised.

"It's winter. But there is a bird!"

The Teacher wrote about the Bird. The story was in the newspaper.

"Tonight I will go to the warm

place," said the Bird.

The Bird went to all the good places. The Bird met other birds. The other birds sang songs. The Bird had a good time.

At night, the Bird flew to the Happy Prince.

"I am leaving," said the Bird.

"Bird, stay with me. Stay with me for one more night," said

the Prince.

"My friends are waiting for me in the warm place," said the Bird. "My friends will fly to the river. There are hippos, big statues, and lions at the river."

"Bird," said the Prince. "In the city, there is a young man. He is at a desk. There are papers and flowers on the desk. His hair is brown. His lips are red. He has big eyes. He is trying to write.

But he is too cold. He is also very hungry."

"I will stay one more night. I can take him a red stone," said the Bird.

"I don't have a red stone now. But I have my eyes. My eyes are blue stones. Take my eye to the young man," said the Prince.

"Prince, I can't do that," the Bird cried.

"Bird, do what I say," said the

Prince.

The Bird took out the stone. The Bird flew to the young man's house. The Bird went into the room. The young man was sleeping. When he woke up, he found the stone.

"Someone left this stone for me. Now I can finish writing," said the young man.

He looked very happy.

Chapter 6

The Little Match-girl

In the morning, the Bird went

to the seaside. The Bird saw the boats.

"I'm going to the warm land!" said the Bird.

At night, the Bird flew to the Happy Prince.

"Goodbye," the Bird said.

"Bird, stay with me. Be with me for one more night," said the Prince.

"It is winter. The snow is coming. The sun is warm in the warm place. My friends are making a house. Prince, I will go. I will come back in spring," said the Bird.

"There is a girl in the city. She sells matches. But the matches are wet. She is crying. Take my other eye. Give it to her," said the Happy Prince.

"I will stay one more night. But I can't take your eye.

You won't see anything," said
the Bird.

"Bird, do what I say," said the
Prince.

So the Bird took out the eye.
The Bird went to the girl. The
Bird put the stone in her hand.

"This is a beautiful
stone," said the
little girl.

She ran home. She was happy.

Then the Bird went back to the Prince.

"You can't see anything. I will stay with you," said the Bird.

"No, Bird. You must go to the warm land," said the Prince.

"I will stay with you forever," said the Bird.

The Bird was near the Prince's feet. The Bird slept.

Chapter 7

The Gifts for the Poor People.

The next day, the Bird told stories to the Prince.

The Bird told him about the warm place. The Bird told him about red birds. The Bird told him about a lion statue. The Bird told him about a King and a green snake.

"Bird, you told me great things. But people have great

stories, too. Go to the city. Tell me about the people," said the Prince.

The Bird went to the city. The Bird saw the rich people. The Bird saw the poor people.

The rich people were happy.
The rich people were in a
house.

The poor people were outside.
The children were cold and
hungry.

Then the Bird came back. The Bird told the Prince about the city.

"I have a golden body. Take my gold. Give it to the people. People think gold is good," said the Prince.

The Bird took the gold. The Bird gave it to the poor people. The Happy Prince had no gold now. But the people were happy.

Chapter 8

The Death of the Swallow

The snow came. The streets were white. People wore warm clothes. Children played on the ice.

The Bird was very cold. But the Bird stayed with the Prince. The Bird loved the Prince.

The Bird was going to die. He went to the Prince.

"Goodbye, Prince! Can I kiss your hand?" said the Bird.

"I am happy that you are going to the warm land. Kiss me on the lips. I love you," said the Prince.

"I am not going to the warm place. I am going to Heaven," said the Bird.

The Bird kissed the Happy Prince on the lips. Then the Bird died.

Then there was a sound. The Happy Prince's heart broke. The Happy Prince died too.

In the morning, the City Leader was walking with the Town Leaders. They saw the statue.

"The Happy Prince looks bad!" the City Leader said.

"He looks bad!" said the Town Leaders.

"The red stone on the sword is gone. His eyes are gone. His gold is gone. He is like a poor person!" said the City Leader.

"Yes! That's right!" said the Town Leaders.

"And here is a dead bird!" said

the City
Leader.

"Tell all the
people. Birds can't die here."

They took away the statue of
the Happy Prince.

"The Happy Prince is not beautiful," said the Art Teacher.

Then people put the Happy
Prince in the fire.

"Let's make another statue. A statue of me!" said the City Leader.

"This is strange. This broken heart is not melting in the fire. Throw it away," said the workman.

So they threw away the heart.

God spoke to His Angel.
"Give me the most beautiful things in the city," said God.

The Angel gave Him the dead heart and the dead bird.

"You are right. This bird will sing forever in heaven. The Happy Prince will be happy forever in heaven," said God.

5 Steps English
The Happy Prince

LEVEL 3

3,127개

단어(Words)

393개

문장수(Sentences)

12분 30초

읽는 시간(Reading Time)

24분 3초

말하는 시간(Speaking TIme)

8.0

문장 길이(Sentence leangth)

Chapter 1

The Happy Prince is Loved

There was a statue high above the city on a pillar. This was the statue of the Happy Prince.

He was covered with gold. He had two bright blue gems for eyes and a big red ruby on his sword.

People loved the Happy Prince very much.

"He is as beautiful as a wind signal," said one of the Town Leaders.

The Leader wanted to show people

that he knew something about art.

"But he is useless," he said. He wanted to look sensible.

"Be like the Happy Prince," said a mother.

Her son was crying because he was wishing for something he could not have.

"The Happy Prince never cries," she said.

A sad man looked at the statue of the Happy Prince.

"I am happy there is someone who is really happy," he said.

The children came out of the church.

"He looks just like an angel," said the children.

They were wearing red and white clothes. These children did not have parents and they lived at the church.

"How do you know?" said the Math Teacher, "you have never seen an angel before."

"Ah! We have seen an angel in our dreams," answered the children.

The Math Teacher made an un-friendly face. The Math Teacher did not want the children to dream.

Chapter 2

The Little Swallow and the Reed

One night, a little Swallow bird flew over the city. His friends flew away to Egypt, but he did not go with them.

He was in love with a beautiful Reed. He met her in spring when he was flying over the river. He loved her pretty waist, and he stopped to talk to her.

"May I love you?" said the Swallow, who wanted to speak his mind.

The Reed nodded to him. He flew around her, touching the water and making little waves. He showed his love to her, and this continued all through the summer.

"This is a silly couple," sang the other Swallows. "She has no money and too many family members."

This was true. The river was full of

other Reeds. Then, in autumn, the other Swallows flew away.

After they left, the Swallow felt lonely. And the Swallow was getting tired of loving the Reed.

"The Reed never talks to me," he said, "and she likes the wind more than me."

This was true. Whenever the wind blew, the Reed waved back and forth in the breeze.

"The Reed is always at home, but I love traveling. I want my wife to love traveling, too. Will you come away with me?" he said to her.

But the Reed shook her head to say, "No." She loved her home too much.

"You tricked me," he cried.
"I will leave for the Pyramids.
Goodbye!" and he flew away.

Chapter 3

The Little Swallow and the Happy Prince

The Bird flew all day, and he came to the city at night.

"Where can I stay?" he said. "I hope the town has a good place for me."

Then he saw the statue on the pillar.

"I will stay there," he said. "It is a good place with fresh air."

So he sat between the Happy Prince's feet.

"My bedroom is made of gold," the Bird said to himself.

The Bird went to sleep. But when the Bird put his head down, some water fell on him.

"This is strange!" he said. "There are no clouds in the sky. The stars are bright. But it is raining. The weather is really bad here. The Reed liked the rain, but she was selfish."

Then some water fell on him again.

"This statue is useless. I do not want to get wet," he said. "I want to find a better place." He was about to fly away.

But before the Bird opened his wings, some water fell on him again. The Swallow looked up and saw something. What did he see?

The Happy Prince was crying. His eyes were full of tears. His face was so beautiful. The Swallow was sad to see the Happy Prince.

"Who are you?" he said.
"I am the Happy Prince."

"Why are you crying then?" asked the Swallow. "You made me very wet."

"When I was alive, I did not know what it felt like to be sad. I lived in a palace. It was not sad in the palace. In the daytime, I played with my friends in the garden. In the evening, I danced in the palace hall. There was a tall wall in the garden, but I never asked what was outside the wall. Everything about me was so beautiful. My helpers called me the Happy Prince. If fun and happiness are the same thing, I was happy. I lived this way, and then I died. Now I am dead and they put me up here.

Now I can see the sad things and the bad things in my city. My heart is dead, but I am still crying," said the statue.

Chapter 4

The Ruby from the Sword

"I thought he was gold," thought the Swallow.

He could not say this out loud.

"Far away," said the statue. "Far away, on the street, there is a poor house. The window is open. I can see a woman at a table. Her face is thin. She has red hands. She has been hurt by her sewing needle. She works all day sewing clothes. She is sewing flowers on a fancy dress for another woman to wear at a special party. Her son is in bed. He is sick.

He has a fever. He wants oranges. But his mother has nothing to give him. She can only give him water. He is crying. Swallow, Swallow, little Swallow, will you take the ruby out of my sword and bring it to her? I can't move my feet. My feet are stuck on this pillar."

"My friends are waiting for me in Egypt," said the Swallow. "My friends are flying up and down the Nile River. They are talking to the flowers on shore. They sleep in the King's grave at night. The King is lying there in a box. There is a yellow cloth over the king's body.

He smells like special spices. He has a green necklace. His hands are very dry."

"Swallow, Swallow, little Swallow," said the Prince. "Will you stay with me for one night? Be my messenger. The boy is so thirsty. The mother is so sad."

"I don't like boys," answered the Swallow. "I was on the edge of the river last summer. There is a man there who makes flour. He has two bad boys. The boys always threw stones at me. But the stones never hit me. I fly very fast. My family is very famous. We all fly very fast. But those boys were very rude to me."

But the Happy Prince looked so sad. The little Swallow felt bad for him.

"It is very cold here," he said. "But I will stay with you for one night. I will be your messenger."

"Thank you, little Swallow," said the Prince.

The Swallow took out the ruby from the Prince's sword. The Swallow flew away with the ruby. The Swallow flew through the town.

He flew by the church tower. He saw white angel statues. He went by the palace. He heard the sound of dancing. A beautiful young woman was with a young man.

"The stars are wonderful," the young man said. "The power of love is wonderful."

"I want my dress to be ready for the special party soon," said the woman. "A woman is sewing flowers on my dress. But she is so slow."

He flew over the river and he saw the lamps on the ships. He flew over the town and he saw the people at the shops.

Finally, he came to the poor house and he looked inside. The boy was sick in bed. The mother was sleeping. The Swallow put the ruby down on the table. Then he flew around the bed. He fanned the boy's face.

"I feel cool. I must be getting better," said the boy.
The boy fell asleep.

The Swallow flew back to the Happy Prince. The Swallow told him what he did.

"It is so cold, but I feel warm now," said the Swallow.

"That is because you did something good," said the Prince.

And the Swallow fell asleep.

Chapter 5

The Sapphire from the Eye

In the morning, the Swallow flew down to the river and he had a bath.

"This is strange," said the Science Professor. He was walking over the bridge. He saw the bird.

"It is winter, but there is a swallow!"

He wrote a story about the bird in the newspaper. Everyone talked about the story.

"Tonight I will go to Egypt," said the Swallow, and he was very excited.

He went to all the famous places in the town. He sat on top of the church for a long time. When he

flew around, the Sparrows sang.

"He is elegant," the Sparrows said.

The Swallow had a good time. At night, the Swallow flew back to the Happy Prince.

"Do you have any requests for me in Egypt? I am ready to go," he said.

"Swallow, Swallow, little Swallow, will you stay with me for one more night?" said the Prince.

"My friends are waiting for me in Egypt," said the Swallow. "My friends will fly up to the river tomorrow. The hippos like to take a rest there. The god Memnon sits on a stone pillar. He watches the stars at night. In the morning, he is happy. He shouts one time. The yellow lions come to the river at 12 p.m. The lions have green eyes, and they have loud voices."

"Swallow, Swallow, little Swallow," said the Prince. "Far away in the city, I see a young man in an attic room. He is at a desk. The desk is covered with papers. There is a cup next to him. There are purple flowers inside the cup. His hair is dry and brown. His lips are red as fruit. He has large, bright eyes. He is trying to finish writing a drama. He is writing a drama for the leader of the theater. But he is too cold to

write any more."

"I will wait with you for one more night," said the Swallow.

The Swallow had a good heart.

"Do you want me to take him a ruby?"

"Oh no! I don't have a ruby now," said the Prince. "I only have my eyes. They are blue gems. The blue gems are from India. They are from a long time ago. Take out one blue gem and give it to the young man. He will sell it."

"Dear Prince," said the Swallow. "I can't do that." He started to cry.

"Swallow, Swallow, little Swallow," said the Prince, "Do what I am asking you."

So the Swallow took the Prince's eye. He flew away to the young man's attic room. It was easy to go in. There was a hole in the roof.

The Swallow flew into the room. The young man was sleeping at the desk. He did not hear the bird.

When he woke up, he found the beautiful blue gem on the dry flowers.

"Someone must love my writing. This must be from a fan. Now I can finish my drama," he said.

He looked very happy.

Chapter 6

The Little Match-girl

The next day, the Swallow flew to the port. He sat on a big ship. He watched the seamen working.

"One, two, three, lift!" the seamen shouted.

"I am going to Egypt!" called the Swallow. But no one cared.

At night, the Swallow flew back to the Happy Prince.

"I came to say goodbye," he said.

"Swallow, Swallow, little Swallow, will you stay with me for one more night?" said the Prince.

"It is winter," answered the Swallow. "The cold snow will come soon. The sun is warm in Egypt. The animals love to rest in the mud. My friends are making a nest in a special place. The pink and white birds are watching my friends and singing. Dear Prince, I need to go. But I will remember you. I will give you two beautiful stones next spring. The ruby will be a deep red color, and the blue gem will be a deep blue color."

"In the city center," said the Happy Prince. "There is a little match-girl. She dropped her matches in the drain, and they are all wet. Her father will hit her if she does not make money. She is crying. She does not have shoes or stockings. And she does not have a hat to wear. Take out my other eye and give it to her. Then her father will not hit her."

"I will stay with you one more night," said the Swallow. "But I can't take out your eye. You would not be able to see anything then."

"Swallow, Swallow, little Swallow," said the Prince, "do what I ask."

So he took out the Prince's other eye, and flew down to the city. He flew past the match-girl, and he put the stone in her hand.

"This is a lovely stone," said the little girl.

The little girl laughed as she ran home.

Then the Swallow came back to the Prince.

"You can't see anything now," he said, "so I will always stay with you."

Chapter 7

The Gifts for the Poor People

The next day, the Bird told him stories about the warm place. The red birds stay along the Nile River. The red birds catch goldfish. The lion statue lives in the desert. He is so old and he knows everything. The traders walk with their camels. They hold yellow bracelets. The King of the Mountains of the Moon prays to a large stone. The great green snake sleeps under a palm tree and eats honey cakes. Small people sail over a big lake on large leaves and butterflies are all around them.

"Dear little Swallow," said the Prince, "you told me about amazing things, but people have amazing stories too. The sad stories about people are a mystery. No one knows why people have pain in life. Fly over my city, little Swallow, and tell me what you see there."

So the Swallow flew over the city. The Bird saw rich people. The rich people were having a big party. But the poor people were sitting outside. The Swallow went into the streets and he saw the hungry children. Under a bridge, there were two little boys lying on the ground.

"We are so hungry!" they said.

"Get out," shouted the Guard. The little boys ran outside.

Then the Swallow flew back and told the Prince what he saw.

"I am covered with gold," said the Prince. "Take it off, and give it to the poor people. People always think that gold can make them happy."

The Swallow took off the gold, layer after layer. He gave the gold to the poor people, layer after layer. Then the children's faces looked happy. They laughed and played in the street.

"We can have food now!" they said.

But the Happy Prince had no more gold on his body. He became ugly.

Chapter 8

The Death of the Swallow

Then the snow came down. The ice came too. The streets looked like silver. They were so bright and shiny.

Long ice was on the edge of the roofs. The ice on the roofs looked like swords.

Everybody wore fur coats. The little boys wore red caps and played on the ice.

The poor little Swallow was very cold. But he did not leave the Prince. The Swallow loved him.

He took pieces of bread from the bakery when the baker was not watching. He moved his wings to stay warm.

After a while, the Swallow knew that he was going to die. He flew up to the Prince's shoulder.

"Goodbye, dear Prince!" he murmured. "Let me kiss your hand."

"I am happy that you are finally going to Egypt, little Swallow," said the Prince. "You stayed here for too long. But you must kiss me on the lips, because I love you."

"I am not going to Egypt," said the Swallow. "I am going to Heaven.

Sleep will send me to Heaven, right?"

He kissed the Happy Prince on the lips, and died at his feet.

Then there was a strange sound inside the statue. The Prince's heart broke into two pieces. It was a very cold winter.

The next morning the City Leader was walking with the Town Leaders in the city center. The City Leader looked up at the statue when they were walking next to the pillar.

"Oh my goodness! The Happy Prince looks so dirty!" he said.

"Yes! He looks so dirty!" said the Town Leaders.

They always copied the City Leader. They looked at the statue.

"The ruby on the sword has come out, his eyes are gone, and he is not golden anymore," said the City Leader, "he is worse than a poor person!"

"Yes, worse than a poor person," said the Town Leaders.

"And here is a dead bird!" continued the City Leader. "We must make a new rule. Birds can't die here."

The Town Worker wrote down the new rule. So they took down the statue of the Happy Prince.

"The Happy Prince is not beautiful; he is useless," said the Art Teacher.

They melted the statue in a fireplace.

The City Leader had a meeting.

"What should we do with this metal?" the people said.

"We should make another statue, of course," the City Leader said, "it will be a statue of me."

"Yes! A statue of me!" said the other people. They had a fight about the statue. They are still fighting with each other now.

"How strange!" said the manager of the workers at the fireplace. "This broken heart is not melting in the fire. Let's throw it away."

So they threw it away with the garbage. The dead Swallow was in the garbage too.

"Bring to me the most wonderful things in the city," said God to his Angel.

And the Angel brought to Him the dead heart and the dead bird.

"Yes. You are right," said God. "In my garden of Paradise, this little bird will sing forever. In my city of gold, the Happy Prince will worship me."

5 Steps English
The Happy Prince

LEVEL 4

3,484개

단어(Words)

329개

문장수(Sentences)

13분 56초

읽는 시간(Reading Time)

26분 48초

말하는 시간(Speaking TIme)

10.6

문장 길이(Sentence leangth)

LEVEL 4

행복한왕자 레벨4

Chapter 1

The Happy Prince is Loved

High above the city, on a tall pillar, stood the statue of the Happy Prince.

He was coated all over with thin layers of gold. For eyes, he had two bright sapphires. A large red ruby was on his sword, and it was shining.

He was very respected.

"He is as beautiful as a wind vane," commented one of the Town Councillors. The Councillor wanted to become famous for having artistic tastes. "He's not very useful, though," he added.

He feared that people would think he was unrealistic.

"You should be like the Happy Prince," said a realistic mother.

Her little boy was crying because he was wishing for impossible things.

"The Happy Prince never thinks about crying for anything."

"I am glad there is someone in the world who is really happy," mumbled a discouraged man as he looked at the wonderful statue.

"He looks just like an angel," said the Orphans as they came out of the church, wearing their red capes and their white aprons.

"How do you know?" said the Math Teacher, "you have never seen one."

"Ah! But we have seen an angel in our dreams," answered the Orphans.
The Math Teacher frowned and looked very serious. He did not allow children to dream.

Chapter 2

The Little Swallow and the Reed

One night, a little Swallow flew over the city. His friends had gone away to Egypt six weeks ago, but he had stayed behind because he was in love with the most beautiful Reed.

He had met her early in the spring when he was flying over the river, chasing a yellow moth. He was drawn to her thin waist, and he stopped to talk to her.

"Shall I love you?" said the Swallow. He was very frank, and the Reed bowed low. The Swallow flew around her, touching the water with his wings and making ripples. This was their love affair, and it continued all through the summer.

"This is a silly engagement," tweeted the other Swallows. "She has no money and too many relatives."

The river was really quite full of other Reeds. Then, when the autumn came, the other Swallows flew away.

After they had gone, he felt lonely and began to grow tired of his love for the Reed.

"She cannot communicate," he said, "and I think she is a flirt. She always plays with the wind."

And sure enough, whenever the wind blew, the Reed made the most beautiful waves.

"I understand that she is homely," he

continued, "but I love traveling, and my wife, of course, should love traveling also."

"Will you come away with me?" he finally said to her.

But the Reed shook her head. She was too connected to her home.

"You were unfaithful to me," he cried. "I will leave for the Pyramids. Goodbye!" and he flew away.

Chapter 3

The Little Swallow and the Happy Prince

He flew all day long, and he arrived in the city at nighttime.

"Where shall I stay?" he said. "I hope the town has a place for me to stay."

Then he saw the statue on the tall pillar.

"I will stay up there," he cried. "It is a fine spot, with lots of air."

So he landed just between the feet of the Happy Prince.

"I have a golden bedroom," he said to himself as he looked around.

He was ready to go to sleep. But when he put his head under his wings, a big drop of water fell on him.

"What a strange thing!" he cried. "There is not a single cloud in the sky, the stars are clear and bright, but it is raining. The weather in Europe is really awful. The Reed used to like the rain, but she was selfish."

Then another drop of water fell.

"This statue is useless if it cannot protect me from the rain," he said. "I must find a chimney," and he decided to fly away.

But before he had opened his wings, another drop of water fell. And he looked up, and saw something. Ah! What did he see?

The eyes of the Happy Prince were filled with tears. The tears were rolling down his golden cheeks. His face looked so beautiful in the moonlight. The little Swallow felt sorry for him.

"Who are you?" he said.

"I am the Happy Prince."

"Why are you crying then?" asked the Swallow. "You have soaked me with tears."

"When I was alive and had a heart," answered the statue, "I did not know what tears were because I lived in the Palace of Sans-Souci, where there was no sadness. In the daytime, I played with my comrades in the garden, and in the evening I hosted parties and danced in the Great Hall. There was a very tall wall around the garden, but I never cared enough to ask what was beyond it. Everything about me was so beautiful. My servants called me the Happy Prince. If delight and happiness are the same, I was happy. So I lived, and so I died. And now, since I am dead, they left me up here so that I can see all the pain and all the sadness of my city. Even though my heart is metal, I cannot do anything but weep."

Chapter 4

The Ruby from the Sword

"What? Is he not pure gold?" said the Swallow to himself. But he was too kind. He could not share his thoughts out loud.

"Far away," continued the statue in a low voice, "far away on a little street, there is a poor house. One of the windows is open, and I can see a woman at a table. Her face is thin and white, and she has rough, red hands. Her hands were injured many times by her sewing needle. She sews clothes for a living. She is sewing flowers on a silk dress for one of the Queen's special guests to wear at the next royal celebration. In the corner of the room, her little boy is sick in bed. He has a fever, and he is asking for oranges. His mother has nothing to give him but river water, so he is crying. Swallow, Swallow, little Swallow, Will you bring her the ruby out of my sword? My feet are attached to this pillar and I can't move."

"My friends are expecting me in Egypt," said the Swallow. "My friends are flying up and down the Nile River, and talking to the large flowers. They will go to sleep soon in the tomb of the King. The King is lying there in a painted casket. He is covered in yellow cloth and preserved with special spices. There is a light green necklace around his neck. His hands are like dry leaves."

"Swallow, Swallow, little Swallow," said the Prince, "will you not stay with me for one night, and be my messenger? The boy is so thirsty, and the mother is so sad."

"I don't think I like boys," answered the Swallow. "I was staying on the river last summer. There were two bad boys there. Their father is the miller. They always threw stones at me. They never hit me, of course. We swallows fly too well for that. My family is famous because we can fly fast. But still, it was disrespectful."

But the Happy Prince looked so sad that the little Swallow felt sorry for him.
"It is very cold here," he said. "But I will stay with you for one night, and be your

messenger."

"Thank you, little Swallow," said the Prince.

So the Swallow pulled out the ruby from the Prince's sword. He flew away with it in his mouth over the houses of the town.

He passed by the church tower. White angel statues were standing there. He passed by the palace and heard the sound of dancing. A beautiful young woman came out on the veranda with her suitor.

"The stars are wonderful," he said to her, "and the power of love is wonderful."

"I hope my dress will be ready for the ball soon," she said. "I asked a woman to sew flowers on the dress. But she is so lazy."

He flew over the river and saw the lamps hanging on the poles of the ships. He flew over the Jewish district and saw the Jewish people buying and selling items. They balanced their money on brown scales.

Finally, he came to the poor house and looked inside. The boy was sick and he was stirring in his bed. The mother had fallen asleep. She was so tired The Swallow jumped inside the window and left the ruby on the table next to the woman's

sewing cap. Then he flew around the bed,
fanning the boy's face with his wings.

"I feel so cool. I must be getting better,"
said the boy.
The boy fell into a deep sleep.

Then the Swallow flew back to the Happy
Prince, and he told him what he had
done.

"It is strange," he said, "it is so cold, but
I feel very warm now."

"That is because you have done a good deed," said the Prince.

And the little Swallow started to think, and then he fell asleep. Thinking always made him sleepy.

Chapter 5

The Sapphire from the Eye

In the morning, he flew down to the river and had a bath.

"What a rare event," said the Professor of Bird Science as he was walking over the bridge. "A swallow in the winter!"

He wrote a long story about it in the town newspaper. Everyone talked about the Professor's story, but they could not understand the big words he used.

"Tonight I will go to Egypt," said the Swallow, and he was thrilled.

He visited all the public places, and sat for a long time on top of the roof of the church.

Wherever he went, the Sparrows sang, and said to each other, "What an impressive visitor!" He enjoyed the time very much.

At night, he flew back to the Happy Prince.

"Have you any orders for me in Egypt?" he cried. "I am about to go."

"Swallow, Swallow, little Swallow," said the Prince, "will you not stay with me for one more night?"

"My friends are expecting me in Egypt," answered the Swallow. "Tomorrow my friend will fly up to the Second Cataract. The river-horse lies down there among the reeds. The god Memnon sits there on a limestone seat. All night long, he watches the stars. In the morning, he shouts for joy one

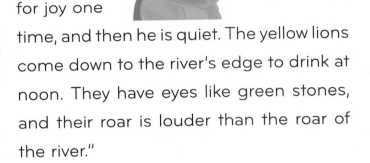

time, and then he is quiet. The yellow lions come down to the river's edge to drink at noon. They have eyes like green stones, and their roar is louder than the roar of the river."

"Swallow, Swallow, little Swallow," said the Prince. "Far away across the city, I see a young man in an attic room. He is bent over a desk. The desk is covered with papers, and in a cup next to him, there are many dry violet flowers. His hair is brown and crisp, his lips are as red as a pomegranate, and he has dreamy eyes. He is trying to finish a play for the Manager of the Theater, but he is too cold to write any more. There is no fire in the heater. The young man is weak with hunger."

"I will wait with you one night longer," said the Swallow.

He really had a good heart. "Should I take him another ruby?"

"Oh, no! I have no ruby now," said the Prince. "My eyes are the only things I have. They are made of special sapphires. They are from India, from one thousand years ago. Pull out one of them and take it to him. He will sell it and buy food and firewood. He will finish his play."

"Dear Prince," said the Swallow. "I can't do that," and he began to cry.

"Swallow, Swallow, little Swallow," said the Prince, "Do as I tell you."

So the Swallow pulled out the Prince's eye, and flew away to the young man's attic room.

It was easy to enter, because there was a hole in the roof. Through the hole he went, and he came into the room. The young man's head was resting in his hands, so he did not hear the sound of the bird's wings.

When he looked up, he found the beautiful sapphire on the dry violet flowers.

"I am beginning to be recognized," the young man cried. "This is from a supporter. Now I can finish my play," and he looked truly happy.

Chapter 6

The Little Match-girl

The next day, the Swallow flew down to the port. He sat on the pole of a large ship. He watched the seamen moving big boxes out of the ship with ropes.

"Heave-ho!" they shouted as each box came up.

"I am going to Egypt!" cried the Swallow. But nobody listened.

At night, he flew back to the Happy Prince.

"I came to tell you goodbye," he cried.

"Swallow, Swallow, little Swallow, will you stay with me for one more night?" said the Prince.

"It is winter," answered the Swallow. "The cold snow will be here soon. In Egypt, the sun is warm on the green trees and the crocodiles lie in the mud and look around. My friends are building a nest in the Temple of Baalbek. The pink and white doves are watching them, and singing to each other. Dear Prince, I must leave you, but I will never forget you. Next spring, I will give you two beautiful stones like the ones you gave away. The ruby will be redder than a red rose. The sapphire will be as blue as the great sea."

"In the plaza below," said the Happy Prince. "There is a little match-girl. She dropped her matches in the ditch, and they are all ruined. Her father will beat her if she does not give him some money, and she is crying. She has no shoes or stockings. And she does not have a hat on her little head. Pull out my other eye. Give it to her, and her father will not beat her."

"I will stay with you one more night," said the Swallow. "But I cannot pull out your eye. You would be blind."

"Swallow, Swallow, little Swallow," said the Prince, "do as I tell you."

So he pulled out the

Prince's other eye, and flew down to the city with it. He rushed past the match-girl, and left the jewel in her hand.

"What a lovely piece of glass," cried the little girl.

She ran home, laughing.

Then the Swallow came back to the Prince.

"You are blind now," he said, "so I will stay with you always."

"No, little Swallow," said the Prince, "you must go away to Egypt."

"I will stay with you always," said the Swallow.

He slept at the Prince's feet.

Chapter 7

The Gifts for the Poor People

All the next day, he sat on the Prince's shoulder and told him stories of the strange lands. He told him of the red ibises, who stand by the Nile River and catch goldfish in their beaks. He told him of the Sphinx, who is as old as the world itself, lives in the desert, and knows everything. He told him of the merchants. They walk slowly next to their camels and carry yellow beads in their hands. He told him of the King of the Mountains of the Moon. The King is as black as black wood and he praises a large crystal. He told him of the great green snake that sleeps in a palm tree, and has twenty ministers who give him honey cakes. He told him of the pygmies who sail over a big lake on large flat leaves. They are always at war with the butterflies.

"Dear little Swallow," said the Prince, "you tell me surprising things, but more surprising than anything is the pain of people. There is no mystery that is bigger than pain. Fly over my city, little Swallow, and tell me what you see there."

So the Swallow flew over the great city, and he saw rich people having parties. But the beggars were sitting at the gates, asking for food. He flew into the dark streets, and saw the pale faces of hungry children. The children looked out at the dark streets. They were so weak. Under the gate of a bridge, two little boys were lying in each others' arms to keep warm.

"We are so hungry!" they said.

"You cannot sleep here," shouted the Warden, and the boys ran out into the rain.

Then he flew back and told the Prince what he had seen.

"I am covered with fine gold," said the Prince. "You should take it off, layer by layer. Give it to my poor people. People always think that gold can make them happy."

The Swallow peeled off the fine gold, layer after layer. Then the Happy Prince looked very bland and grey.

He brought the fine gold to the poor

people, layer after layer. The children's faces turned to a rosy pink color, and they laughed and played games in the street.

"We can have bread now!" they cried.

Chapter 8

The Death of the Swallow

Then the snow came. After the snow, the frost came. The streets looked like they were made of silver. They sparkled brightly. Long ice crystals hung from the roofs of the houses. They looked like crystal blades. Everybody went around wearing furs, and the little boys wore red caps and skated on the ice.

The poor little Swallow grew colder and colder, but he would not leave the Prince. He loved him very much. He gathered bread crumbs outside the baker's shop when the baker was not looking. He tried to keep himself warm by fluttering his wings.

At last, the Swallow knew that he was going to die. He only had a little strength to fly up to the Prince's shoulder one more time.

"Goodbye, dear Prince!" he murmured, "will you let me kiss your hand?"

"I am pleased that you are going to Egypt at last, little Swallow," said the Prince, "you have stayed too long here. But you must kiss me on the lips, because I love you."

"It is not to Egypt that I am going," said the Swallow. "I am going to the House of Death. Death comes after Sleep, right?"

He kissed the Happy Prince on the lips, and fell down dead at his feet.

At that time, there was a strange noise inside the statue. It sounded like something had broken. The Prince's heart had broken right in two. It really was a terribly cold winter.

Early the next morning, the Mayor was walking with the Town Councillors in the plaza below. When they passed the pillar, he looked up at the statue.

"Oh my! The Happy Prince looks so worn out!" he said.

"Yes, really! Very worn out!" cried the Town Councillors, who always agreed with the Mayor. They went up to look at the statue.

"The ruby has come out of his sword, his eyes are gone, and he is not golden anymore," said the Mayor, "he is worse than a beggar!"

"Yes, worse than a beggar," said the Town Councillors.

"And look at this! There is a dead bird at his feet!" continued the Mayor.

"We must make an announcement. Birds are not free to die here."

The Town Clerk made a note.

So they took down the statue of the Happy Prince.

"He is not beautiful anymore, so he is not useful anymore," said the Art Professor at the University.

They melted the statue in a kiln, and the Mayor met with the town council to decide what to do with the metal.

"We must have another statue, of course," he said," and it should be a statue of myself."

"Oh yes, a statue of myself," said each of the Town Councillors, and they argued. The last time I heard about them, they were still arguing with each other.

"What a strange thing!" said the manager of the workmen at the kiln factory. "This broken metal heart will not melt in the fire. We must throw it away."

So they threw it in the rubbish pile. The

dead Swallow was also lying there.

"Bring me the two most valuable things in the city," said God to one of His Angels.

The Angel brought Him the metal heart and the dead bird.

"You chose the right ones," said God," for in my garden of Paradise, this little bird will sing forever, and in my city of gold, the Happy Prince will praise me."

5 Steps English
The Happy Prince

LEVEL 5

3,546개
단어(Words)

228개
문장수(Sentences)

14분 11초
읽는 시간(Reading Time)

27분 16초
말하는 시간(Speaking TIme)

15.6
문장 길이(Sentence leangth)

Chapter 1

The Happy Prince is Loved

High above the city, on a tall column, stood the statue of the Happy Prince. He was gilded all over with thin leaves of fine gold; for eyes, he had two bright sapphires, and a large red ruby glowed on his sword-hilt.

He was very much admired indeed. "He is as beautiful as a weathervane," remarked one of the Town Councillors who wished to gain a reputation for having artistic tastes; "only not quite so useful," he added, fearing lest people should think him impractical, which he really was not.

"Why can't you be like the Happy Prince?" asked a sensible mother of her little boy who was crying for the moon. "The Happy Prince never dreams of crying for anything."

"I am glad there is someone in the world who is quite happy," muttered a disappointed man as he gazed at the wonderful statue.

"He looks just like an angel," said the Charity Children as they came out of the cathedral in their bright scarlet cloaks and their clean white pinafores.

"How do you know?" said the Mathematical Master, "you have never seen one."

"Ah! But we have, in our dreams," answered the children, and the Mathematical Master frowned and looked very severe, for he disapproved of children dreaming.

Chapter 2

The Little Swallow and the Reed

One night there flew over the city a little Swallow. His friends had gone away to Egypt six weeks before, but he had stayed behind, for he was in love with the most beautiful Reed. He had met her early in the spring as he was flying down the river after a big yellow moth, and had been so attracted by her slender waist that he had stopped to talk to her.

"Shall I love you?" said the Swallow, who liked to come to the point at once, and the Reed made him a low bow. So he flew round and round her, touching the water with his wings and making silver ripples. This was his courtship, and it lasted all through the summer.

"It is a ridiculous attachment," twittered the other Swallows; "she has no money, and far too many relations"; and indeed the river was quite full of other Reeds. Then, when the autumn came, they all flew away.

After they had gone, he felt lonely and began to tire of his lady-love.

"She has no conversation," he said, "and I am afraid that she is insincere, for she is always flirting with the wind." And certainly, whenever the wind blew, the Reed made the most graceful curtseys. "I admit that she is domestic," he continued, "but I love traveling, and my wife, consequently, should love traveling also."

"Will you come away with me?" he said finally to her, but the Reed shook her head; she was so attached to her home.

"You have been trifling with me," he cried. "I am off to the Pyramids. Goodbye!" and he flew away.

Chapter 3

The Little Swallow and the Happy Prince

All day long he flew, and at night-time he arrived at the city. "Where shall I put up?" he said; "I hope the town has made preparations."

Then he saw the statue on the tall column.

"I will put up there," he cried; "it is a fine position, with plenty of fresh air." So he alighted just between the feet of the Happy Prince.

"I have a golden bedroom," he said softly to himself as he looked round, and he prepared to go to sleep; but just as he was putting his head under his wing a large drop of water fell on him. "What a curious thing!" he cried; "there is not a single cloud in the sky, the stars are quite clear and bright, and yet it is raining. The climate in the north of Europe is really dreadful. The Reed used to like the rain, but that was merely her selfishness."

Then another drop fell.

"What is the use of a statue if it cannot keep the rain off?" he said; "I must look for a good chimney-pot," and he determined to fly away.

But before he had opened his wings, a third drop fell, and he looked up, and saw—Ah! What did he see?

The eyes of the Happy Prince were filled with tears, and tears were running down his golden cheeks. His face was so beautiful in the moonlight that the little Swallow was filled with pity.

"Who are you?" he said.

"I am the Happy Prince."

"Why are you weeping then?" asked the Swallow; "you have quite drenched me."

"When I was alive and had a human heart," answered the statue, "I did not know what tears were, for I lived in the Palace of Sans-Souci, where sorrow is not allowed to enter. In the daytime, I played with my companions in the garden, and in the evening I led the dance in the Great Hall. Round the garden ran a very lofty wall, but I never cared to ask what lay beyond it, everything about me was so beautiful. My courtiers called me the Happy Prince, and happy indeed I was, if pleasure be happiness. So I lived, and so I died. And now that I am dead they have set me up here so high that I can see all the ugliness and all the misery of my city, and though my heart is made of lead yet I cannot choose but weep."

202

Chapter 4

The Ruby from the Sword

"What? Is he not solid gold?" said the Swallow to himself. He was too polite to make any personal remarks out loud.

"Far away," continued the statue in a low, musical voice, "far away on a little street there is a poor house. One of the windows is open, and through it I can see a poor woman seated at a table. Her face is thin and worn, and she has coarse, red hands, all pricked by the needle, for she is a seamstress. She is sewing passion -flower decorations on a satin gown. This gown is for one of the most lovely guests of the Queen. This special guest will wear the gown at the next royal ball. In a bed in the corner of the room the poor woman's boy is lying ill. He has a fever, and is asking for oranges. His mother has nothing to give him but river water, so he is crying. Swallow, Swallow, little Swallow, will you not bring her the ruby out of my sword-hilt? My feet are fastened to this pedestal and I cannot move."

"Friends are expecting me in Egypt," said the Swallow. "My friends are flying up and down the Nile, and talking to the large lotus-flowers. Soon they will go to sleep in the tomb of the great King. The King is there himself in his painted coffin. He is wrapped in yellow linen, and embalmed with spices. Around his neck is a chain of pale green jade, and his hands are like withered leaves."

"Swallow, Swallow, little Swallow," said the Prince, "Will you not stay with me for one night, and be my messenger? The boy is so thirsty, and the mother so sad."

"I don't think I like boys," answered the Swallow. "Last summer, when I was staying on the river, there were two rude boys, the miller's sons, who were always throwing stones at me. They never hit me, of course; we swallows fly far too well for that, and besides, I come from a family famous for its agility; but still, it was a mark of disrespect."

But the Happy Prince looked so sad that the little Swallow was sorry.

"It is very cold here," he said; "but I will stay with you for one night, and be your messenger."

"Thank you, little Swallow," said the Prince.

So the Swallow plucked out the great ruby from the Prince's sword, and flew away with it in his beak over the roofs of the town.

He passed by the cathedral tower, where the white marble angels were sculptured. He passed by the palace and heard the sound of dancing. A beautiful girl came out on the balcony with her lover. "How wonderful the stars are," he said to her, "and how wonderful is the power of love!"

"I hope my dress will be ready in time for the State-ball," she answered; "I have ordered passion -flowers to be embroidered on it; but the seam-stresses are so lazy."

He passed over the river, and saw the lanterns hanging on the masts of the ships. He passed over the Ghetto, and saw the old Jews bargaining with each other, and weighing out money on copper scales. At last he came to the poor house and looked in. The boy was tossing feverishly on his bed, and the mother had fallen asleep, she was so tired. He hopped, and laid the great ruby on the table beside the woman's thimble. Then he flew gently round the bed, fanning the boy's forehead with his wings. "How cool I feel," said the boy, "I must be getting better"; and he sank into a delicious slumber.

Then the Swallow flew back to the Happy Prince, and told him what he had done. "It is curious," he remarked, "but I feel quite warm now, although it is so cold."

"That is because you have done a good action," said the Prince. And the little Swallow began to think, and then he fell asleep. Thinking always made him sleepy.

Chapter 5

The Sapphire from the Eye

When day broke, he flew down to the river and had a bath. "What a remarkable phenomenon," said the Professor of Ornithology as he was passing over the bridge. "A swallow in winter!" And he wrote a long letter about it to the local newspaper. Everyone quoted it; it was full of so many words that they could not understand.

"Tonight I go to Egypt," said the Swallow, and he was in high spirits at the prospect. He visited all the public monuments, and sat a long time on top of the church steeple. Wherever he went the Sparrows chirruped, and said to each other, "What a distinguished stranger!" so he enjoyed himself very much.

When the moon rose, he flew back to the Happy Prince. "Have you any commissions for Egypt?" he cried; "I am just starting."

"Swallow, Swallow, little Swallow," said the

Prince, "Will you not stay with me one night longer?"

"Friends are expecting me in Egypt," answered the Swallow. "Tomorrow my friends will fly up to the Second Cataract. The river-horse couches there among the bulrushes, and on a great granite throne sits the god Memnon. All night long he watches the stars, and when the morning star shines, he utters one cry of joy, and then he is silent. At noon, the yellow lions come down to the water's edge to drink. They have eyes like green beryls, and their roar is louder than the roar of the cataract."

"Swallow, Swallow, little Swallow," said the Prince, "Far away across the city I see a young man in a garret. He is leaning over a desk covered with papers, and in a tumbler by his side there are a bunch of withered violets. His hair is brown and crisp, and his lips are red as a pomegranate, and he has large and dreamy eyes. He is trying to finish a play for the Director of the Theater, but he is too cold to write any more. There is no fire in the grate, and hunger has made him faint."

"I will wait with you one night longer," said the Swallow, who really had a good heart. "Shall I take him another ruby?"

"Alas! I have no ruby now," said the Prince; "My eyes are all that I have left. They are made of rare sapphires, which were brought out of India a thousand years ago. Pluck out one of them and take it to him. He will sell it to the jeweler, buy food and firewood, and finish his play."

"Dear Prince," said the Swallow, "I cannot do that." And he began to weep.

"Swallow, Swallow, little Swallow," said the Prince, "Do as I command you."

So the Swallow plucked out the Prince's eye, and flew away to the young man's garret. It was easy enough to get in, as there was a hole in the roof. Through this he darted, and came into the room. The young man had his head buried in his hands, so he did not hear the flutter of the bird's wings, and when he looked up he found the beautiful sapphire lying on the withered violets.

"I am beginning to be appreciated," he cried. "This is from some great admirer. Now I can finish my play," and he looked quite happy.

Chapter 6
The Little Match-girl

The next day the Swallow flew down to the harbor. He sat on the mast of a large vessel and watched the sailors hauling big chests out of the hold with ropes. "Heave a-hoy!" they shouted as each chest came up. "I am going to Egypt!" cried the Swallow, but nobody minded, and when the moon rose he flew back to the Happy Prince.

"I came to bid you goodbye," he cried.

"Swallow, Swallow, little Swallow," said the Prince, "Will you not stay with me one night longer?"

"It is winter," answered the Swallow, "and the chill snow will soon be here. In Egypt the sun is warm on the green palm trees, and the crocodiles lie in the mud and look lazily about them. My companions are building a nest in the Temple of Baalbek, and the pink and white doves are watching them, and cooing to each other. Dear Prince, I must leave you, but I will never forget you, and next spring I will bring you back two beautiful jewels in place of those you have given away. The ruby shall be redder than a red rose, and the sapphire shall be as blue as the great sea."

"In the square below," said the Happy Prince, "There stands a little match-girl. She has let her matches fall in the gutter, and they are all spoiled. Her father will beat her if she does not bring home some money, and she is crying. She has no shoes or stockings, and her little head is bare. Pluck out my other eye, and give it to her, and her father will not beat her."

"I will stay with you one night longer," said the Swallow, "but I cannot pluck out your eye. You would be quite blind then."

"Swallow, Swallow, little Swallow," said the Prince, "do as I command you."

So he plucked out the Prince's other eye, and darted down with it. He swooped past the match-girl, and slipped the jewel into the palm of her hand. "What a lovely bit of glass," cried the little girl; and she ran home, laughing.

Then the Swallow came back to the Prince. "You are blind now," he said, "so I will stay with you always."

"No, little Swallow," said the poor Prince, "you must go away to Egypt."

"I will stay with you always," said the Swallow, and he slept at the Prince's feet.

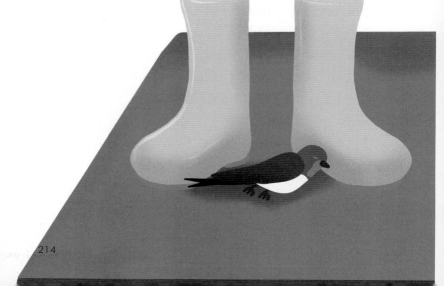

Chapter 7

The Gifts for the Poor People

All the next day he sat on the Prince's shoulder, and told him stories of what he had seen in strange lands. He told him of the red ibises, who stand in long rows on the banks of the Nile, and catch gold-fish in their beaks; of the Sphinx, who is as old as the world itself, and lives in the desert, and knows everything; of the merchants, who walk slowly by the side of their camels, and carry amber beads in their hands; of the King of the Mountains of the Moon, who is as black as ebony, and worships a large crystal; of the great green snake that sleeps in a palm tree, and has twenty priests to feed it with honey-cakes; and of the pygmies who sail over a big lake on large flat leaves, and are always at war with the butterflies.

"Dear little Swallow," said the Prince, "you tell me of marvelous things, but more marvelous than anything is the suffering of men and of women. The misery of people is a mystery. No one knows why people suffer. Fly over my city, little Swallow, and tell me what you see there."

So the Swallow flew over the great city, and saw the rich making merry in their beautiful houses, while the beggars were sitting at the gates. He flew into dark lanes, and saw the white faces of starving children looking out listlessly at the black streets. Under the archway of a bridge two little boys were lying in one another's arms to try and keep themselves warm. "How hungry we are!" they said. "You must not lie here," shouted the Watchman, and they wandered out into the rain.

Then he flew back and told the Prince what he had seen.

"I am covered with fine gold," said the Prince, "you must take it off, leaf by leaf, and give it to my poor; the living always think that gold can make them happy."

Leaf after leaf of the fine gold the Swallow

picked off, till the Happy Prince looked quite dull and grey. Leaf after leaf of the fine gold he brought to the poor, and the children's faces grew rosier, and they laughed and played games in the street. "We have bread now!" they cried.

Chapter 8

The Death of the Swallow

Then the snow came, and after the snow came the frost. The streets looked as if they were made of silver, they were so bright and glistening. Long icicles like crystal daggers hung down from the eaves of the houses, everybody went about in furs, and the little boys wore scarlet caps and skated on the ice.

The poor little Swallow grew colder and colder, but he would not leave the Prince, he loved him too well. He picked up crumbs outside the baker's door when the baker was not looking and tried to keep himself warm by flapping his wings.

But at last he knew that he was going to die. He had just enough strength to fly up to the Prince's shoulder once more. "Goodbye, dear Prince!" he murmured, "will you let me kiss your hand?"

"I am glad that you are going to Egypt at last, little Swallow," said the Prince, "you have stayed too long here; but you must kiss me on the lips, for I love you."

"It is not to Egypt that I am going," said the Swallow. "I am going to the House of Death. Death is the brother of Sleep, is he not?"

And he kissed the Happy Prince on the lips, and fell down dead at his feet.

At that moment a curious crack sounded inside the statue, as if something had broken. The fact is that the leaden heart had snapped right in two. It certainly was a dreadfully hard frost.

Early the next morning, the Mayor was walking in the square below in company with the Town Councillors. As they passed the column, he looked up at the statue: "Dear me! how shabby the Happy Prince looks!" he said.

"How shabby indeed!" cried the Town Councillors, who always agreed with the Mayor; and they went up to look at it.

"The ruby has fallen out of his sword, his eyes are gone, and he is golden no longer," said the Mayor in fact, "he is little better than a beggar!"

"Little better than a beggar," said the Town Councillors.

"And there is actually a dead bird at his feet!" continued the Mayor. "We must really issue a proclamation that birds are not to be allowed to die here." And the Town Clerk made a note of the suggestion.

So they pulled down the statue of the Happy

Prince. "As he is no longer beautiful he is no longer useful," said the Art Professor at the University.

Then they melted the statue in a furnace, and the Mayor held a meeting of the Corporation to decide what was to be done with the metal. "We must have another statue, of course," he said, "and it shall be a statue of myself."

"Of myself," said each of the Town Councillors, and they quarreled. When I last heard of them, they were still quarreling.

"What a strange thing!" said the overseer of the workmen at the foundry.

"This broken lead heart will not melt in the furnace. We must throw it away." So they threw it on a dust-heap where the dead Swallow was also lying.

"Bring me the two most precious things in the city," said God to one of His Angels; and the Angel brought Him the leaden heart and the dead bird.

"You have rightly chosen," said God, "for in my garden of Paradise this little bird shall sing for evermore, and in my city of gold the Happy Prince shall praise me."